Love for rent

Michael Jarvis

BookLeaf Publishing

India | USA | UK

Presentation by *BookLeaf Publishing*

Web: www.bookleafpub.com

E-mail: info@bookleafpub.com

ISBN: 9789358313048

First edition 2023

ACKNOWLEDGEMENT

A big thank you to Roberta, Alaina, Louis, Rachel and everyone at wfc, colm, Danny, Gemma, and everyone who has supported me in this project. Also to Cait Barlow for the picture clover.

Last summer mornings

Watching birds fishing in the lake
Some of these things you can not fake
Taking time to reflect on days to make
Clouds are clearing above the lake

Mistakes are only regrets made in haste
Embraced lovers on a interstate
Empty heads with a mindless waste
Looking for signs at a wildness lake
Broken bottles let open beside

Summer solstice on a summers day
Following thoughts into a gathering
Breathing clear air with a following
Dreaming of a friend with a sorrowing
Ducks feeding by a greasy overflow
Tell me beauty, how dose it feel

Writing poems by morning sunrise
Some guys running by breaks of dawn
Looking for words to rhyme in a carbon haze
Picking up your legs on a dirty maze
Open roads have a lot to say
Tell me girl what's to say

Out of my league

But I'm so into you
I'm getting into you like glue
I want to be with you
Like I'd want to stick to a paper tattoo
And we are not just two
Cos I'm getting into you

I'd have a take away with you
A Chinese and a side a few
But not the one with a bad review
I'd order everything for you
Apart from a chicken Chow Mein
For two

But I feel like I'm punching above with you
Your out of my league it's true
And I don't know to stay
Or call myself out and walk away
But you'll understand that I'm real for you
Real for you like too

I wish I could cuddle n spoon with you
And watch fun shows in the mood with you
Drink larger and apple beer with you
We could order a film for two

We could get matching tattoos on our backs It's
true
 it hurts but not as much
As being without you when you're over the pain
it's true
A love heart and a few years faded link
We can just not talk about it till its a fade

I wanna cuddle up with you
Like a couple should do
And be in bed till noon
Drinking tea till teatime too soon

I want to keep your hoodie
cos it's smalls blue of you
Like I like your scent it's you

See Thunder and lighting with you
Watch the clouds flash up in the sky
But I'm too shy to say I'm sacred
When I'm not with you
Am Finding it hard to stay to sleep without you

Demons and Dragons

We shouldn't feel any shame
I just want you to say my name
Say my name as a lover as a hunter
We Shouldn't feel no blame

Iw slay your dragon if you kill my demons
Wave the white flag
cos we have furious reasons
Seasons greetings Christmas heating

Iw slay your dragon and leave my demons
Iw stay where it's dungeons and demons
Mormans and reasons just happened to reason

Iw slay your dragon and you kill my demons
Stay as my woman and iw give you a reason Iw
save your dreams
hold your nightmares
An let you be carefree

Iw slay your dragon as I feel a reason for me
stay and that I love you

Iw slay your dragon as you have killed my
demons

If the music plays forever
Our stars will shine together
I thought we would always be together
You and I

If 5 were 6
And 6 were 7
I'd be with you right till heaven

You are

The everything and nothing
That something that I always wanted

You are the most beautiful
The most beautiful girl
That I've ever witnessed

You are the one that I always wished for
That I've always kept looking for
Kept looking for yesterday

You are the understanding one
Understanding one that understands
Life can't stand still standing still

You are the one I love
The only one only love
Love is worth waiting for,

Roll back

Roll back the sun sets
Let our hearts return
Forgot about our concerns
Won't get our fingers burned
This time we have learnt
Do we need to wait for the spark to return?

Think back to before our heartache
When we would share a milkshake
And all that mattered when
We both made a earthquake
On my bedroom floor
And you just wanted more

Bring back the times when we went walking
To nowhere and back
To see how much we could chat
About things that would make us relax
And you told me that I always made you climax

Back in the days when we was
Lost and poor
We always known we would have more
Now our love is like a prisoner of war
Now i work at a general store

And your no longer on the dance floor

Roll back to days past
Roll back to loves last days

Let me be

Let me be me
Let me be free
To be who I want to be
Be it good or bad
Gay or straight
Left or right
Right to wrong
Let me sing my own song

Let me be someone
I want someone to fall in love with
Let me be something to be proud of
Let me learn how to ride a bike
Leave me to make my mistakes
To leave all the fakes
Swim this lake

Let me live my life
Let me find my wife

Untitled

Give me a date
And give me a time
Give me a reason
And give me a ryham
Another day
Another time
Life is just a unique crime

Give me a reason
Give me a smile
Give me a sign
Hope should leave our mind
Another day
Another way
Life is just a hopeless grime

Love for rent

My love isn't for rent
Or for lease
My love is real for you to keep
For you to antique

My love isn't for sale
Or for hire
My love is forever
For you to endeavour

My love isn't second hand
Or is it part exchange
My love is sacred
For my soul mate to care

My love isn't cheap
It's here for keep

Love for rent

For Roberta

Castles in the clouds

Love me lots lollipops
Cup of tea in a coffee shop
On a tabletop with a soda pop
As the record stops
We kissed goodbye
As the air takes in the first show drop

Was we making castles in the clouds
Or just dreaming out loud
Lost and found
We never looked down
Turnaround

Forgot me nots
Sugar pots lie on a empty desktop
We past the pawnshop by the co-op
Traffic builds as we hold hands
Dreaming about making plans
Listening to our favourite bands

Was we making castles in the clouds
Or just dreaming out loud
Lost and found
We never looked down
Turnaround

Love and romance

Love and romance
Tired and won't dance
Let's stay at home
Have another chance

Hate and devotion
From years of emotion
True feelings are
Open like a ocean

Pride and tried
Love is blind
Like April Skye's
And heaven decides

Hopes and fears
In these real tears
Is making me hear
Suspicious to clear

Love and romance
And I don't know if I should stay
And do the right thing
Only the best will do
For your love
And our romance

November lights

On a autumn winters night
We cuddled to the light
The light was just enough
To see our eyes glazed through love
A hangover haze of fashion
That lights out nights passion
The rain begins a new action
The rain begins the mornings
In perfect satisfaction
Until the clouds start a reaction
Our eyes in a chain reaction
Over the physical attraction
That night's midnight action
That nights passion
That nights love

Without you

Like a fair without rides
Wedding with no bride
An legs without feet
I'm a empty seat

Like a cat without a mouse
A door without a house
Liverpool with no scouse
Sunday plate without spouts
A concert without touts

A toad with no hole
A car with no patrol
Music an no rock n roll
Toilet with no roll
American with gun control
Without you I've no heart and soul

A footballer and no team
A thief with no scheme
A cinema without a screen
A cowboy with no jeans
With out you I've no dreams

Gold glitters

Like gold glitters
Pears fickler
An the light begins to linger
Your love moves like a finger
My fingertips begin to shiver
Have my soul for dinner
Winner winner chicken dinner
Not getting any thinner
Love begins to dimmer
If only for lucy pinder
My heart starts to timber
Good job I'm a swimmer
Ich bin ein Berliner
Love is nearer
If I'm to linger
Let the lights fickler tonight
So I can make her desire quiver
Like her gold glitters

Penny for your thoughts

A penny for your thoughts
Iw hold your words in court
Be up and forth
Head to the north
Done come apart
As you hold my heart
This is our fresh start
As we head south and depart

Penny for your thoughts
I just want to hear your words
Be up close and true
I'm here for you
You have my heart
Can I be your restart
As we never will be apart

Christmas

What I wouldn't do to have
Christmas time with you
Christmas tree with lights
A snowy sight, Turkish delight
Moonlight kiss under the mistletoe
After glow of the years past

Hot chocolate burning on a stove
Fairy tales from a treasure trove
Returning laughter for what one knows

I don't want to be singing
Whams last Christmas
What i would to give for you
this Christmas

Long shadows

Was I just a picture on your wall
Or sex against your bathroom door
A memory to keep for you to adore
Someone less for me to bore

Didn't i show you the right dedications
Did it not meet your expectations
All the wrong temptations
A school for thought
And a sweet sensation

Wasn't my love enough for you to break
A promise to make a heart to fake
Wasn't i smart enough to partake
In your only heartbreak

You took me in and spat me out
I sincerely doubt you'll Hear me out

What do I have to do

What do I have to do
To show i truly do
That I really do love you

What words can I say
To make you come away
Let us get our love underway

What do I have to do
To shine my light
And get it into you
That I really want you

How many poems can I write
To get my words out to you
I'm the one for you

Why can't we just
Go away for a week or two
In the sun a cocktail or room for two

When we can show
Each other are love
And not be distant lovers
Forgotten summers
Not leave anything under covers

Some love

Wouldn't it be nice to have
someone to be with
someone to hang with
someone to talk with
someone to spend romantic weekends with
someone to share a life with someone to be safe
with and feel secure with

Somebody who won't care if I cry
Over silly and stupid things
Somebody who will always support
Somebody I can court
Somebody who will let me be me
And won't let me be they or them

Something that we can hold
And to have and to keep from cold
Something that is worth more then gold
To be told the world is our behold

Someone who will share her
Most personal stories
Someone who won't vote Tory's
An share all my glories

Someone who will tell me when
I'm right or wrong or incorrect
Help me recollect
Almost living in a world of law in effect
A world we both respect

Someone I can love
Someone I can adore
Someone I'w always be wanting more
And hope to never bore
And more definitely never ignore

3 colours

All my feelings dressed in black
I know your love is not coming back
Looked at the mirror and seen
My reflection looking back
He said Mike you got to take your life back
Your going down a road you cant hack
Sitting a ride you need to sack
Stop looking back at what you cant unpack

All my feelings feeling blue
I look at at you an your leaving too
screaming and believing it's true
You say "I got to get out we are though"
Staying is like being in a zoo with you
Who knew it would be so downhill
Astonishing how we are still grounded
When we are always so clouded

All my feelings turning a green envy
Remember how to be friendly
said "men can be every woman's enemy"
I'm no Ron Jeremy just Mike with a memory
But your on my mind quite heavily
I can't believe I've lost you to my jealousy
Whoever he is he better be heavenly
Especially now I'w never be helplessly
Over you

Mis Luna 1989

As I walk down this open goal
Reminiscing and missing
All the faces, voices of years gone past
Some are still here
Same are just a memory
But one face is shining
More then most
A voice that never leaves or lowers tone
A face that hides no beauty
Or shows no shadow

So tell me why of all the stars I've ever seen
There is but one who shires every night
Like a candie flickering in a stormy night
Like the sun shining on a cloudy day
There is one star who always shires
Come rain and find me
Mis Luna 1989

If the sky is blue and water is clear
And faces appear under what is near
Then why why do we fear what disappears
Houses and fixtures hold souvenirs
And memories of flavours
Leaves on the ground bring no favours
All sailors lead me to
Mis Luna 1989

21 Nights

21 nights
21 dreams
21 schemes
21 bad day dreams
21 themes of loneliness
21 tears of fears
21 night's spent wishing
21 autumn nights wondering where you are

21 days of not knowing
21 days thinking it's me all alone
21 afternoon hours
21 nights over thinking
21 nights too much drinking
21 nights feeling like am shrinking
21 months since you started working

21 midnight suns
21 late night runs
21 coffee run
21 miles to fun town
21 lights in the background
21 highlights in the in the lost and found
21 days waiting for a my text to come round
21 nightmares the tv without sound

21 stairs to get back to the overgrown
21 years since i changed my phone background

21 nights without you alone